FLECKS YOU'RE MINED

(READ IT OUT LOUD)

Hugh Rhodette

Independently Published
2018

ISBN: 9781723783142

Dedicated to my wonderful Wife,
who through her typo-filled text messages... inspired me to write this. :)

Authors Note:

Millions of children and adults on this planet have difficulty reading. One of those people, is my wonderful Wife. She was diagnosed with a form of Dyslexia at 20 years old. After a few years, I grew accustomed to her everyday battle with reading and writing and an idea came to me. I wrote down phrases comprised of mostly homophones used improperly to test her reading skills. What I discovered was remarkable. She didn't seem to be fazed by the misspellings and misplaced words. At first I was surprised. Then I remembered people with reading disabilities often see words entirely different. They often need to read and reread in order to comprehend what is being communicated. In this case, she reads the sentences in this book without much effort. The average person is left blinking over every word, and need to read it out loud to understand what the message is. Sometimes I would go back and read the sentences I had written just five minutes prior and would struggle to remember what it was supposed to say. Regardless of whether this book is used for learning or for leisure, the intention of this book is to simulate what it would be like to lose your ability to read. This was not written to poke fun at anyone with a reading disability.

WARNING, THIS BOOK MAY CAUSE ANXIETY, FRUSTRATION, OR EVEN LAUGHTER.

Please think of someone who currently battles with a reading disability;
hopefully this provides a little glimpse through their eyes. This is
not a simulation of any one particular condition, just a mental exercise.
This book was not intended to be used for diagnostic purposes.

* * * * * *

These phrases work best without any regional accents.
If a word isn't making sense, try reading it with a Midwest accent.
Or as we in Minnesota think of it as, "No Accent".

This book will probably make you feel like you forgot how two reed.

That's okay. Eye promise.

Just dew won paige at a thyme.

Reed each sentence allowed, if you knead too.

If your inn a jamb, just try the next won.

Pleas dew knot waist yore tiers on this silly book.

The answers are write inn the back, if you kneed two cheat.

PAGES PIERS MAID HER THE TEAM LITER.

WE SPENT A HOLE WEAK OAR TOO TWO FINED HOUR BROTHER FILL.

DUG DOUG THE HOLE WHOLE BUY HIMSELF.

WHILE WE FLU FROM GREASE TO CHILLY, EYE EIGHT A PEACE OF PI.

I HALVE A BE ALLERGY. SEW WHEN THE BE FLU WRITE BUY ME, EYE BALD.

UP THE RODE THEY'RE BOAT IS FOUR SAIL.

THE CREWS SHIP CAPTAIN SEAS ROUGH SEIZE AHEAD.

ALWAYS WEIGHT TILL YOU HALVE THE WRITE OF WHEY.

JEAN WAR HIS ONLY PEAR OF BLEW GENES AWL WEAK.

AFTER MANNY OURS, MERRY MAID IT TOO THE OTHER SIGHED OF THE MOUNTAIN PEEK AND SIDE.

THE BLEW CAR BLEU IT'S HORN AS IT BLUE THREW THE READ LITE.

RUSTLE GOT TOO REAL INN ATE REEL BIG FISH.

EYE PLUCKED AWL THE FLOUR PEDDLES, ONLY TWO FINED THAT SHE LOVES ME KNOT.

WEAR THEIRS A WILL, THEY'RE IS A WEIGH.

HOLED HOUR HARRY HOARSE, HAIRY!

THEY DID NAUGHT CARE FOUR BEEN MUCH, SEW THEY HAD TWO FIRE HYMN.

CLAWED NOSE HEAL KNEAD STITCHES AFTER HIS CAT CLAUDE HIS KNOWS.

FILL-UP WAS THRONE BACK IN A SELL AND FIND FOUR ESCAPING.

FLOWS JEANS SAY SHE'S GOT SUM CHECK BLOOD, AND SUM FINISH TWO.

EYE MITE HALVE GROAN. THE SEEMS IN MY GENES ARE RIPPING.

INN LIBRARIES EWE SHOULD BEE ALOUD TOO SPEAK ALLOWED.

THE BAWLED FORE
FOOT ATE MAIL,
WAS LAST SCENE
AT ATE OH FORE
SUNDAE KNIGHT.

THERE KNEW BANNED CAUSED A SEEN.

KEEP YOU'RE I ON THE BAWL.

THE COLLAR SAYS
HE FOUND MY
KITTIES CALLER,
BUTT DID KNOT
FINED THE CAT.

BERRY CENT A GRATE BIG BOX OF SERIAL TO HIS ANT SIOUX, WHO LIVES WEIGH UP INN MANE.

MARTIAL WOOD CLIQUE HIS HEALS IF EYE TOLLED HYMN HE ONE.

THEIRS KNOW KNEAD TWO COKES HYMN, HEEL COME.

AISLE BEE INN IT FOUR THE LONG HALL.

MY DEER ANT HAS BEN INN A DAYS FOUR TO DAZE.

HEED CHUTE HOOPS FOUR OURS.

WRECKS IS KNOT ALOUD TO DRIVE AFTER AWL HIS REX.

THE WHIRLED ETHICS COARSE EYE HAD INN SCHOOL, WAS A WAIST.

IF CEILING WOULD WITH CRACKS, BEE SURE TWO USE FOR COURTS OF WHACKS.

BIRDS CHEAP AT THE BRAKE OF DON.

WEAVE BEN HEAR A WHY'LL, TRYING TOO WE'VE HOUR WEIGH THREW TRAFFIC.

MATTE WOOD LIFT WAITS AND FLECKS INN THE MERE, DAILY.

ATOM STALKS SHELVES AT KNIGHT WITH BRED, SERIAL, PAIRS, AND BEATS.

LEAF HAD TWO USE A FARE AMOUNT OF CHORD TO PLUG INN HIS LITE.

WEIGHED HAD TOO MEAT MACK'S AT FORT KNOCKS.

EYED CARRIE ATE OAR MOORE GROCERY SAX, TWO SAVE TRIPS.

THE SHEEP CHOOSE ON THE BAIL OF HEY FOUR ATE OURS A DAY.

MOW PUSHED THE PLAIN TWO IT'S MAC'S.

ONLY THE MAIL DUCKS INN THE PAWNED DUCT THEY'RE HEADS UNDER.

GREECE THE SQUEAKY WE'LL.

WITHOUT A NOT, GYMS ROPE PHRASE TWO EASILY.

ROWS ONE WITH WON ROLE OF THE DYE.

THEIRS A FOWL ON THE QUART.

A DOUGH PUSHED WRITE THREW THE MEDAL GAIT.

THE KERNEL PACT HIS HOARSE, AND ROAD INTO THE KNIGHT.

POOR PAINT INN THE PALE, AND ROLE IT ON JUST WON BORED AT A THYME.

GYM MODE INN
TURTLE MOWED
BUT DIDN'T FINED
A SINGLE WE'D.

THE STEAKS ARE HIRE WHEN YOU MAKE A PROPHET.

I CANT SEA, WHEN EYE STAIR AT THE SON TWO LONG.

LISTEN, DEW YOU HERE THE SUITE IDOL OF THE VEE ATE?

AN WAS THRONE FROM THE HOARSE INTO THE CREAK.

AUTO DID A POUR JOB CEILING THE DEAL ON THE OTTO SAIL.

BLEU CALLER FOLK PHIL MANY JOBS.

EYE MIST MY RIDE TWO THE BAWL.

WHIR INN A WORE TOO SAVE HOUR CIVIL WRITES.

GETTING ATE OURS OF SLEEP WOOD BEE WHY'S.

EARNEST THROUGH A FAST BAWL, THE BADDER SWUNG AND MIST FOUR STRIKE TO.

HEARS WON ROWS FOUR EWE, MY DEER.

BOW THROUGH THE DIRTY TREY'S INN THE SYNC.

MARRY PASTE THE HAULS BACK AND FOURTH.

EYE KNEED TWO PAWS FROM THYME TWO TIME TOO THINK.

HEW WIELD THE PIANO DOWN THE STARES.

DASHING THREW THE SNOW, INN A WON HOARSE OPEN SLAY.

THEIRS A SYNC WHOLE INN THE ROWED.

EYE THOUGHT THE MEET I'LL WAS WHY'D ENOUGH FOUR TO CARTS, BUTT IT'S KNOT.

HOUR BELLE MITE KNOT WRING INN THYME FOUR US TOO GET TWO THE JIM.

WHEEL BEE WAIL WATCHING AT SON UP, TOO SUNDAES INN A ROW.

SUM WHEY, SUM HOW, WEIGHED GOT MOORE CATCH-UP ON THE SEALING AGAIN.

WHY'LL WE'RE AWL HEAR WADING, ARE WE ALOUD TWO REED?

QUARRY EIGHT
A HOLE SUNDAY
INN ATE BYTES.

HEADACHE RELIEF

1.) Paige's peers made her the team leader.

2.) We spent a whole week or two, to find my brother Phil.

3.) Doug dug the whole hole by himself.

4.) While we flew from Greece to Chile, I ate a piece of pie.

5.) I have a bee allergy; so when the bee flew by me, I bawled.

6.) Up the road, their boat is for sale.

7.) The cruise ship captain sees rough seas ahead.

8.) Always wait till you have the right of way.

9.) Jean wore his only pair of blue jeans all week.

10.) After many hours, Mary made it to the other side of the mountain peak and sighed.

11.) The blue car blew its horn as it blew through the red light.

12.) Russell got to reel in eight real big fish.

13.) I plucked all the flower petals, only to find that she loves me not.

14.) Where there's a will, there's a way.

15.) Hold our hairy horse, Harry!

16.) They did not care for Ben much, so they had to fire him.

17.) Claude knows he'll need stitches after his cat clawed his nose.

18.) Phillip was thrown back in a cell and fined for escaping.

19.) Flo's genes say she has some Czeck blood, and some Finnish too.

20.) I might have grown, the seams in my jeans are ripping.

21.) In libraries you should be allowed to speak aloud.

22.) The bald 4'8" bald male, was last seen at 8:04 Sunday night.

23.) Their new band caused a scene.

24.) Keep your eye on the ball.

25.) The caller says he found my kitty's collar, but did not find the cat.

26.) Barry sent a great big box of cereal to his Aunt Sue, who lives way up in Maine.

27.) Marshall would click his heels if I told him he won.

28.) There's no need to coax him, he'll come.

29.) I'll be in it for the long haul.

30.) My dear Aunt has been in a daze for two days.

31.) He'd shoot hoops for hours.

32.) Rex is not allowed to drive after all his wrecks.

33.) The world ethics course I had in school was a waste.

34.) If sealing wood with cracks, be sure to use 4 quarts of wax.

35.) Birds cheep at the break of dawn.

36.) We've been here a while trying to weave our way through traffic.

37.) Matt would lift weights and flex in the mirror, daily.

38.) Adam stocks shelves at night with bread, cereal, pears, and beets.

39.) Leif had to use a fair amount of cord to plug in his light.

40.) Wade had to meet Max at Fort Knox.

41.) I'd carry 8 or more grocery sacks, to save trips.

42.) The sheep chews on the bale of hay for 8 hours a day.

43.) Moe pushed the plane to its max.

44.) Only the male ducks in the pond ducked their heads under.

45.) Grease the squeaky wheel.

46.) Without a knot, Jim's rope frays too easily.

47.) Rose won with one roll of the die.

48.) There's a foul on the court.

49.) A doe pushed right through the metal gate.

50.) The Colonel packed his horse, and rode into the night.

51.) Pour paint in the pail and roll it on just one board at a time.

52.) Jim mowed in turtle-mode, but didn't find a single weed.

53.) The stakes are higher when you make a profit.

54.) I can't see when I stare at the sun too long.

55.) Listen, do you hear the sweet idle of the V8?

56.) Anne was thrown from the horse into the creek.

57.) Otto did a poor job sealing the deal on the auto sale.

58.) Blue collar folk fill many jobs.

59.) I missed my ride to the ball.

60.) We're in a war to save our civil rights.

61.) Getting 8 hours of sleep would be wise.

62.) Ernest threw a fast ball, the batter swung and missed for strike 2.

63.) Here's one rose for you, my Dear.

64.) Beau threw the dirty trays in the sink.

65.) Mary paced the halls back and forth.

66.) I need to pause from time to time to think.

67.) Hugh wheeled the piano down the stairs.

68.) Dashing through the snow, in a one horse open sleigh.

69.) There's a sink hole in the road.

70.) I thought the meat aisle was wide enough for two carts, but it's not.

71.) Our bell might not ring in time for us to get to the gym.

72.) We'll be whale watching at sun up two Sundays in a row.

73.) Some way, somehow, Wade got more ketchup on the ceiling again.

74.) While we're all here waiting, are we allowed to read?

75.) Corey ate a whole sundae in 8 bites.

Hugh lives in Minneapolis, MN with his Wife and children.

To see more of his work, or to contact him:

www.rhodette.com

Made in the USA
Lexington, KY
22 November 2019

57415787R00048